BOOK ONE

CELEBRATE AMERICA!

MW01130957

A Collection of 10 Late Elementary to Early Intermediate Piano Solos
Reflecting the Beauty, Grandeur and Spirit of America

MARTHA MIER

Foreword

This collection of 10 late elementary to early intermediate solos reflects the beauty, grandeur and spirit of our great country. It was written as a tribute to America in honor of the 500th anniversary of its discovery.

What began as a thin thread of early European adventurers led by Christopher Columbus in 1492 has grown into a rich tapestry of American people. This tapestry is woven with music as diverse and varied as our cultural backgrounds.

The moods and styles of the music in this collection vary from quiet, romantic, dignified melodies to rollicky, happy, carefree tunes; from the country tune of *Texas Bluebonnets* to the patriotic sounds of *Celebrate America!*

It is hoped that students will find pleasure in exploring this music of America. Teachers will find this collection useful in preparing special programs for the quincentennial celebration of America.

Martha Mier

Contents

Alfred

Cover Design: Tanya Maiboroda
Interior Illustrations: Beverly Lazor-Bahr
Boat in harbor, Couple hiking, Mt. McKinley and
Yellowstone Lower Falls: Images ©1996 PhotoDisc, Inc.
Others: Corel Corporation.

New World Discovery

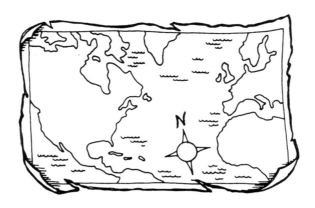

Martha Mier

Fast, festive

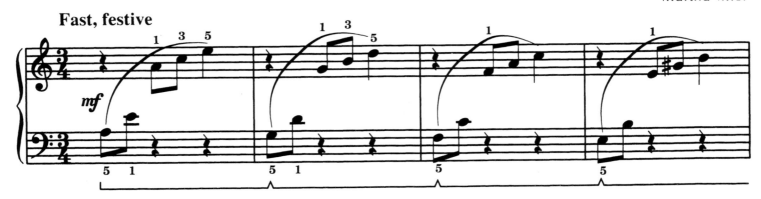

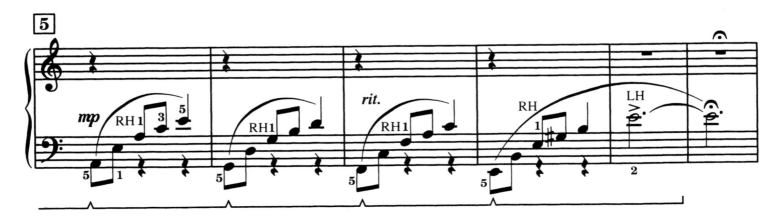

3

4

Smoky Mountain Waterfall

Martha Mier

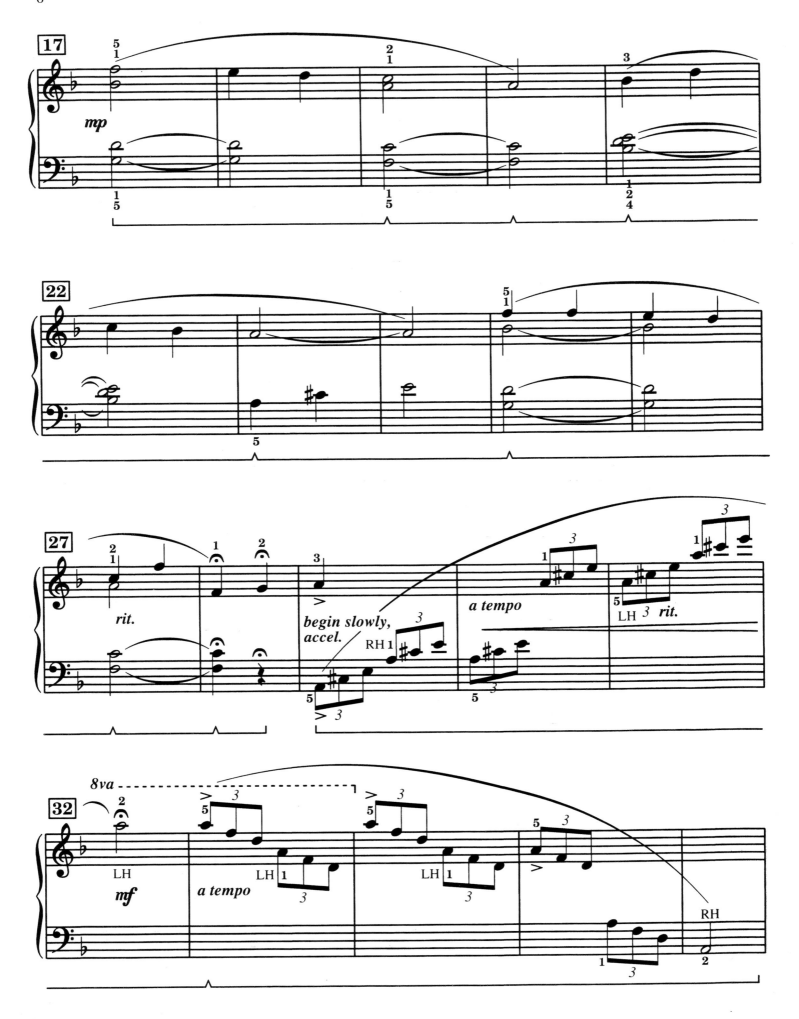

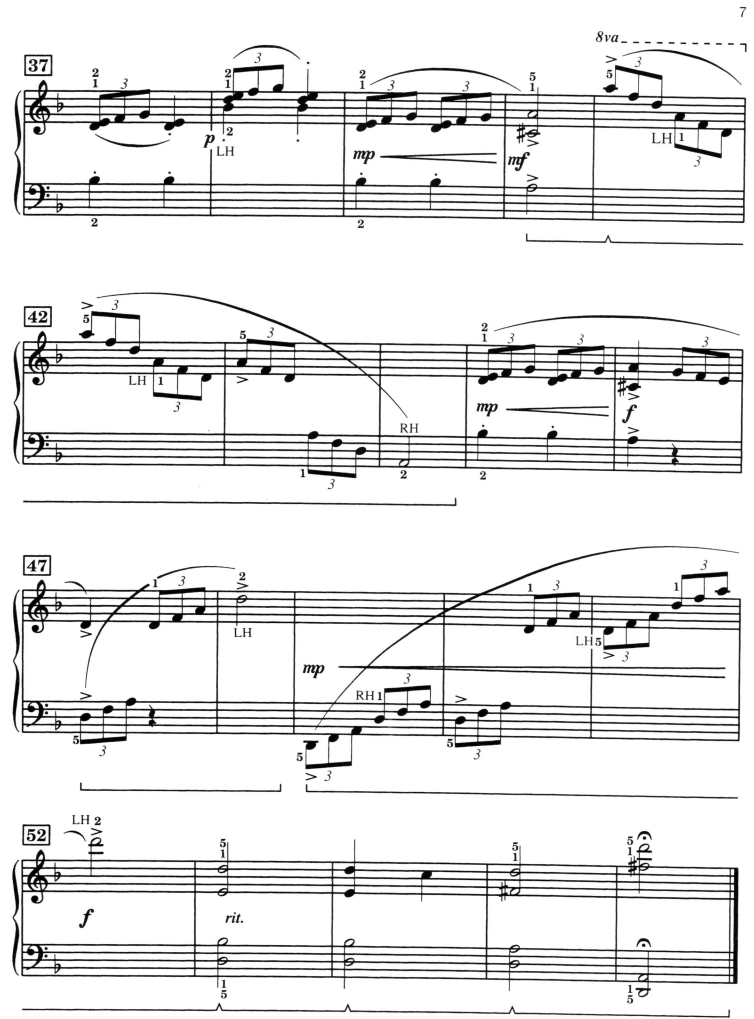

Magnolia Blossoms

Martha Mier

A Cherokee Legend

Martha Mier

Fast, spirited

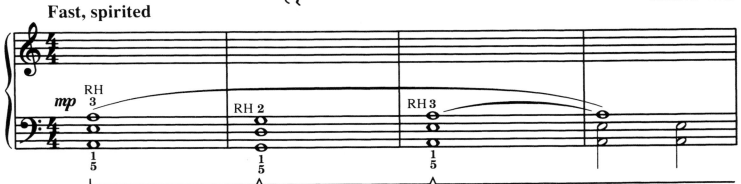

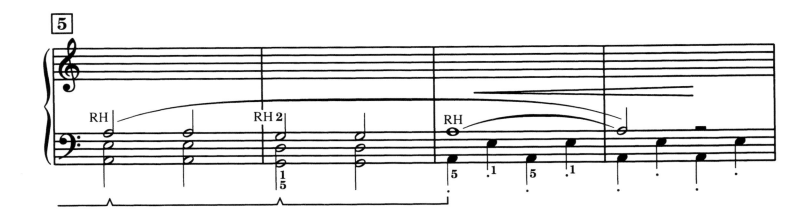

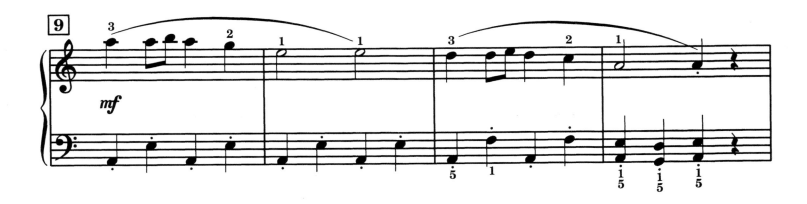

11

Stars Over the Painted Desert

Martha Mier

Tenderly, with expression

Oklahoma Hayride

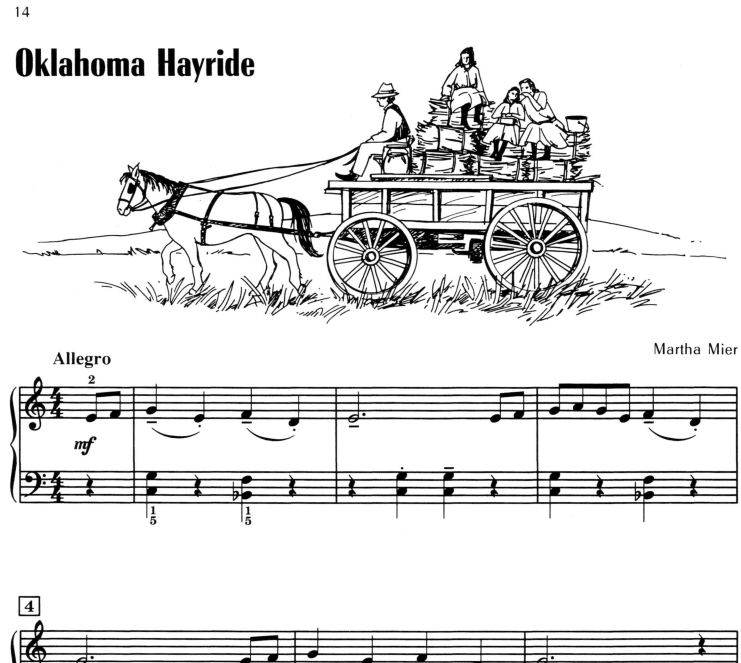

Martha Mier

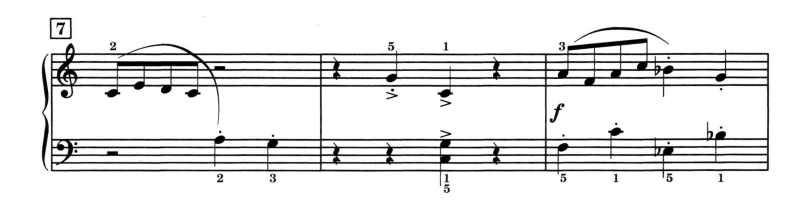

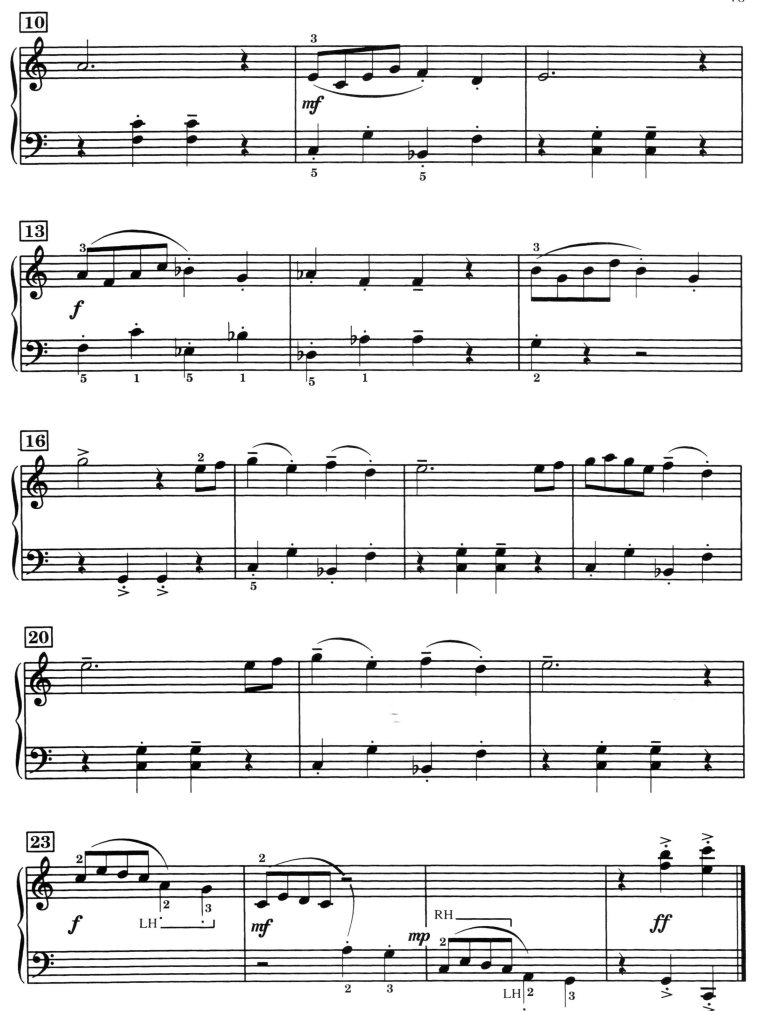

Texas Bluebonnets

Martha Mier

Songs of Faith

(Amazing Grace, Simple Gifts)

Arranged by
Martha Mier

Slowly, with reverence (♩ = 80)

Orange Blossom Rag

Martha Mier

Celebrate America!

(America, the Beautiful)

Arranged by
Martha Mier

Majestically, with dignity (♩ = 84)

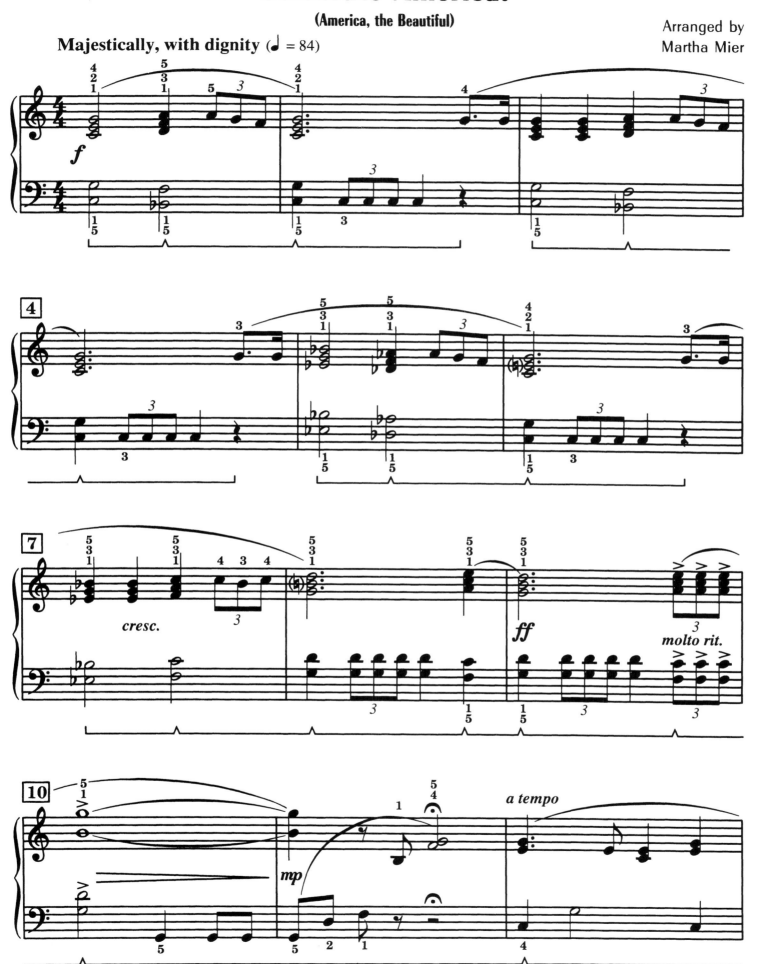